LIFE IN THE
MOUNTAINS

Written by **Catherine Bradley**

Consultant: Roger Hammond
Director of Living Earth

PRINCETON ■ LONDON

Published in the United States and Canada by
Two-Can Publishing LLC
234 Nassau Street
Princeton, NJ 08542

www.two-canpublishing.com

For information on Two-Can books and multimedia,
call 1-609-921-6700, fax 1-609-921-3349, or visit our web site at
http://www.two-canpublishing.com

'Two-Can' is a trademark of Two-Can Publishing.
Two-Can Publishing is a division of Zenith Entertainment plc,
43-45 Dorset Street, London W1H 4AB

hc   ISBN 1-58728-5541
sc   ISBN 1-58728-569X

hc 1 2 3 4 5 6 7 8 9 10 02 01 00
sc 1 2 3 4 5 6 7 8 9 10 02 01 00

Printed in Hong Kong

Photograph Credits:
p.4-5 Bruce Coleman/Dieter & Mary Plage p.7 (top) Bruce Coleman/Steve Kaufman (bottom) Bruce Coleman/C.B. & D.W. Frith p. 8 (left) ZEFA/Ned Gillette (center) London/Ian Beames p.9 (right) Bruce Coleman/Stephen J. Krasemann p.10 (bottom left) Ardea, London/François Gohier (top right) Ardea, London/Kenneth W. Fink (right) Bruce Coleman/Hans Reinhard (bottom right) Survival Anglia/Clive Huggins p.12 Survival Anglia/Jeff Foott p.13 (top) Bruce Coleman/Erwin and Peggy Bauer (bottom) Bruce Coleman/Steve Kaufman p.14 Bruce Coleman/C. B. & D. W. Frith p. 15 (top) Survival Anglia/Richard & Julia Kemp (bottom left) Ardea, London/Eric Dragesco (bottom) Ardea, London/Kenneth W. Fink p.16 (top) Hutchinson Library p. 17 Ardea, London/Richard Waller p.18 (bottom left) Gerald Cubitt p.22 Bruce Coleman/M. P. Price

Front cover: Bruce Coleman/Wayne Lankinen. Back cover: Ardea, London/Eric Lindgren.

Illustrations by Michaela Stewart. Story written by Claire Watts. Edited by Monica Byles.

CONTENTS

All words marked in **bold** can be found in the glossary.

LOOKING AT MOUNTAINS

High above the valleys and plains soar the mighty mountains of the world. Mountains come in many different shapes and sizes. They can be jagged, icy peaks; smoking **volcanoes**; or even green and fertile islands.

A wide and unique variety of animals, plants, and people has adapted to life on steep and rocky slopes. Some insects also live on mountain pastures. A few, like glacier fleas, can even live in ice and snow.

THE HEART OF THE EARTH

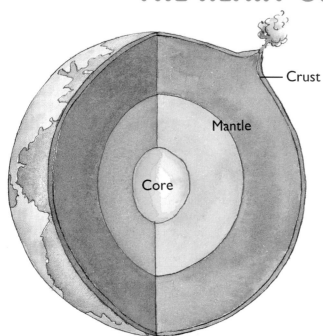

Crust

Mantle

Core

The earth is like an onion, made up of different layers of rock. The center, or **core**, is made up mostly of iron. The next layer is the **mantle**, a tightly packed band of rock about 1,800 miles (2,900 kilometers) thick. We live on the cool, outermost layer, or **crust**. This is up to 30 miles (50 kilometers) thick.

Near the earth's crust, the rocks of the mantle are hot and molten. This liquid rock, or lava, is squeezed from every side. Where the crust is weak, it spews out the lava and forms a type of mountain called a volcano.

Very few mountains rise alone from a plain. Usually they form part of a longer chain, or range, of mountains, such as the Andes, which run the length of the west coast of South America. As the earth's surface changes, new mountains form slowly over millions of years, and older ones gradually wear away.

This book mainly looks at the many different forms of life on the mighty mountains of the world.

▼ Mount Everest in the Himalaya is the highest peak on earth. It is 29,028 feet (8,848 meters) high. The Himalaya is the world's most recently formed mountain range. It is 1,500 miles (2,410 kilometers) long and 2,000 feet (6,000 meters) high, on average.

MAKING MOUNTAINS

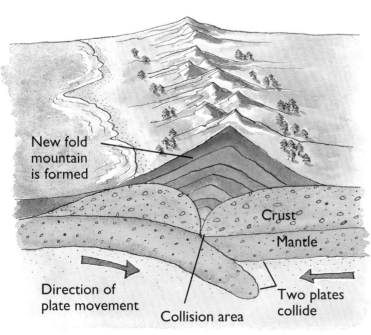

New fold mountain is formed

Crust

Mantle

Direction of plate movement

Collision area

Two plates collide

Large areas of the earth's crust, called **plates**, move slowly around on the earth's surface. The oceans and continents ride on the plates. Long ago, the plates were joined. Their edges could still fit together like pieces of a puzzle.

Sometimes the plates meet and grind together, causing earthquakes. At their edges, the rocks slowly fold upward to form **fold mountains** or drift apart to form valleys.

One plate may make the edge of another plate sink, while the rocks at its own edge rise very slowly to make a new range of mountains.

WHERE IN THE WORLD?

Any area of land that is higher than 1,000 feet (300 meters) above its surrounding flat land can be called mountainous. Mountains cover about one-fifth of the earth's surface. Australia and Africa have only a few mountains, while Asia has huge areas of mountainous land.

Vast mountains also form part of the ocean floor. Hawaii is the topmost part of an underwater volcano. Measured from the sea floor, it is higher than Mount Everest, at more than 29,500 feet (9,000 meters) tall.

Fault-block mountains have broad, flat tops, or **plateaus**. These mountains form when blocks of rock are forced up through cracks, or faults, in the crust by the liquid rock in the mantle. Rift valleys form when rock slides into a crack in the crust.

▼ This map shows the main mountain ranges. The younger ones, the Alps, the Rockies, the Andes, and the Himalaya, are fold mountains. The Scottish Highlands, the Atlas and Appalachian mountains, the Drakensberg, the Urals, and the Pyrenees are older and have been worn by the weather for millions of years.

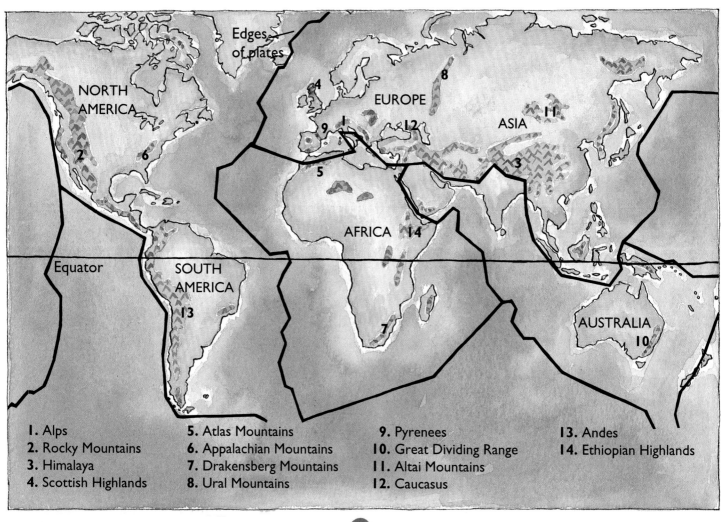

1. Alps
2. Rocky Mountains
3. Himalaya
4. Scottish Highlands
5. Atlas Mountains
6. Appalachian Mountains
7. Drakensberg Mountains
8. Ural Mountains
9. Pyrenees
10. Great Dividing Range
11. Altai Mountains
12. Caucasus
13. Andes
14. Ethiopian Highlands

◀ Mount Augustine is a live volcanic island off the coast of Alaska. In 1986, it erupted, and ash and gases spouted from its crater.

▼ Weird limestone mountains stand near the Guilin Li River in China. Limestone is soft and is worn away gradually by the wind or dissolved by rain. Over the years, these unusual mountains have been ground into strange shapes.

ICE, SNOW, AND RAIN

Mountains change all the time. Over the years, heavy rains soften their rocky outlines and gather to form rivers. These rivers eventually carve deep V-shaped channels or valleys into the side of the mountain.

Ice and snow also change the shape of mountains. There is less air high up a mountain to trap the warmth of the sun's rays, so it is very cold. Many of the world's peaks are covered with a deep blanket of snow and ice throughout the year.

RAIN SHADOWS

Rain-filled clouds blow toward the land from the sea. They release their moisture when they reach cold mountain air. The landward side of a mountain receives little rain and is called the **rain shadow**.

▲ Sometimes snow gets too heavy and slips down the mountainside as an **avalanche**.

▶ Ice may form slow-moving rivers called glaciers. Stones and rocks in the ice **erode**, or wear away, the mountains, leaving U-shaped channels, known as glaciated valleys. The glacier melts as it gets farther from the cold peak and into warmer areas. Shown here is the John Hopkins glacier in Alaska.

▼ Heavy rains often loosen the earth on a mountain and lead to a landslide. Strong winds also may blow away rocks and soil and change a mountain's shape. Sometimes heavy rocks and earth tumble down a mountainside, damaging buildings and injuring people.

TREES AND PLANTS

At high **altitudes**, it becomes harder for mountain plants to survive the cold and lack of water. Completely different plants grow on a protected sunny slope than on a slope exposed to icy winds.

In the Northern Hemisphere, both **deciduous** and **coniferous trees** grow on lower mountain slopes. Farther up, the deciduous trees thin out, and coniferous trees grow more thickly. Beyond, a few coniferous trees struggle to the **treeline**. Above this, conditions are too harsh for trees to grow. The height of the treeline varies with **latitude** and local weather patterns. Mountains away from the **equator** are colder and have lower treelines.

In tropical areas, dense rain forests grow lower down, while lush "cloud" forests of mossy **evergreen trees** grow farther up mountain slopes.

▲ A small ponderosa pine anchors itself in a boulder on a steep mountainside. The waxy needlelike leaves contain very little water to freeze and are shaped so that most snow will slide off the branches and not harm the tree.

◀ Cushions of grass, moss, and lichen grow on the thin soil and rock of upper slopes. At ground level, they are sheltered from the wind. All plant life stops at the **snowline**.

▶ In summer, the meadows high up in the European Alps are covered with a rich carpet of flowers. The plants must be sturdy to combat the cold and windy conditions. They are not very tall and their stems bend in the wind. Their roots hold them firmly in place. The petals are brightly colored to attract the few insects living there.

PLANT PANEL

In the Northern Hemisphere, deciduous and coniferous trees grow on lower slopes. Higher up, only coniferous trees survive. Once past the treeline, only shrubs, grasses, and flowers may grow on the thin mountain soil.

▼ The giant lobelia lives on Mount Kenya. It traps air in its hairs to keep warm. It grows up to 26 feet (8 meters) tall.

STAYING WARM

Mountain animals have long hair with a thick undercoat of fur to keep them warm. They are often larger than their relatives who live in valleys and plains. Some animals, like wild sheep and goats, feed on top pastures in summer and move downhill in winter. Smaller animals, like Alpine marmots and the mountain hares of Europe and Asia, feed mainly in top meadows. Marmots feed all summer and then **hibernate** for eight months and lose as much as one-quarter of their body fat.

Several **predators** stalk the mountains. In the Himalaya, rare snow leopards live near the snowline and prey on grazing animals. In Europe, hunters such as wolves and lynxes are seen occasionally.

▲ Mountain goats have hard, sharp hooves that grip the rock like pincers as they move about slippery top slopes to graze.

ANIMAL FACTS

● Pikas are found on European, Asian, and North American mountains. They feed on grasses and other plants. They spend the summer collecting stores of food to eat during the winter.

● The snow rabbit and the mountain hare both turn white in the winter so as to hide against the snow. This form of protection against predators is called **camouflage**.

▶ The cougar lives close to the snowline during the summer. Cougars, like brown bears and lynxes, prey on goats and other grazing animals.

▼ The Japanese macaque monkeys in the Shiga Highlands have learned to keep warm in the local hot springs. They cook their vegetables in the hot water before eating them. Here, one macaque checks another's fur for ticks and fleas.

FLYING AND HOPPING

The animals living on either side of a mountain range are often quite different from one another. Some birds and insects, however, manage to survive on either side. Birds must have thick feathers and strong lungs to be able to fly so high. Such specially equipped birds include the bar-headed goose, which migrates from Siberia to its distant wintering grounds in India.

The large birds of prey that live close to mountain peaks include the giant Andean condor, the lammergeier, and the golden eagle. There are also smaller birds that remain close to the ground, such as the chough in Europe and Asia, which feeds on insects, butterflies, and mountain plants.

FLYING HIGH

The Apollo butterfly lives on some of the highest mountains of Europe and Asia. It flies only when sunshine warms it. When the sun goes behind a cloud, the Apollo drops to the ground to save energy. The Apollo is now protected by law from butterfly collectors in most of its habitats in Europe.

◀ The mountain grasshopper has stiff flaps where its wings used to be. Those insects, like butterflies, that do still fly, stay near the ground so that they will not be blown away by the wind. Some insects even survive above the snowline.

▶ In the French Pyrenees, a male capercaillie struts about in the snow searching for a mate. Its call is a series of crackles and pops. The capercaillie mainly feeds on buds and cones.

▲ The lammergeier nests in mountain peaks. It is a large mountain vulture native to Europe, Asia, and Africa and mostly feeds on dead animals. Most other birds could not survive the cold.

► The hummingbirds of the high Andes become sluggish when it is cold at night. This is a red-tailed comet hummingbird.

MOUNTAIN DWELLERS

Lowland people get exhausted at high altitudes. There is little oxygen, and it is extremely cold. Mountain people have adapted to these harsh conditions. People such as the Bhotia of the Himalaya have enlarged hearts and lungs and wide nostrils so that their bodies may take in enough oxygen. They depend on sturdy yaks, members of the cattle family, to provide them with meat, wool, milk, transport, hides and butter.

In many areas, such as the Rocky Mountains, the European Alps, and Scandinavia, farmers rear dairy cattle and sheep in the mountains. The animals often are kept in barns on the valley floors to shelter them from the winter snows. In summer, they are herded to the higher pastures to be fattened on the rich grasses.

▲ An Afghan woman dressed in richly colored clothing milks her goat in the Hindu Kush.

▶ A lively market takes place in the Sherpa capital of Namche in Nepal. Sherpas farm, raised animals, and trade. They often act as guides and porters for mountaineering expeditions.

PEOPLE FACTS

● The Lapps are nomads who live in northern Sweden. Some Lapps keep reindeer to provide meat, milk, and skin for tents and clothes.

● The Andean Indians of South America keep llamas, vicunas, and alpacas. Some mine tin, copper, gold, and silver. Others grow barley and potatoes.

MOUNTAIN TREASURES

Valuable resources such as coal, metals such as copper, zinc, and iron ores, as well as semiprecious and precious minerals are mined from mountains. The bare rock itself is used by the building industry.

The banks of the Rocky Mountains in Canada are covered with useful softwoods, such as aspen, pine, and spruce. Hardwoods such as teak, ebony, mahogany, and rosewood grow on tropical mountains. Ships, furniture, and building materials are made from different types of wood.

Mountain rivers are often dammed to feed a reservoir of water. The rushing torrent turns huge turbines, which generate enough electricity to power whole cities or even nations, such as mountainous Switzerland.

▼ A dam is built on the Columbia River in Canada to store water for the use of city-dwellers.

▶ A loader piles logs onto the back of a trailer. When trees are felled on mountain slopes, the rain is no longer absorbed by the roots but runs freely, washing soil into the rivers. In the end, the slopes are left bare and eroded. With proper management, wood can be cut from special plantations.

◀ Emeralds are mined in the Andes in Colombia. The stones are cut and polished to make jewelry.

MOUNTAIN STOREHOUSE

Jewels, such as diamonds, rubies, emeralds, sapphires, quartz, gold, and platinum are taken from minerals and rocks found in mountains.

Granite and marble may be used in building banks, town halls, or palaces. Slate is used for making roofing tiles, and limestone is used to make cement.

Copper, zinc, and iron are extracted from mountain rocks. They are used in construction and sculpture and to make jewelry, tools, and utensils.

Softwoods are important for use in the construction of buildings, to make paper, and as fuel. Hardwoods are used to make long-lasting furniture.

MOUNTAINS IN DANGER

There are many threats to the mountains. Summer visitors can erode paths and crush rare plants. New ski resorts may scar whole mountainsides with cable cars and ski lifts.

Everywhere, mountain forests are being damaged. In many industrial nations, **acid rain** harms mountain forests. Cars and factories produce chemicals that pollute the rain. In Nepal, many trees are felled for fuel. Remaining tree roots cannot absorb enough rain water, so the fertile topsoil washes into the rivers, flooding them downstream. The mountain slopes are left bare, stripped down to their barren rock.

Mining can destroy a mountain, leaving only ugly waste. In Western Australia, entire mountains are dug away to remove their iron ore.

▲ In the Black Forest of southern Germany, mountain trees are poisoned by acid rain. The trees lose their leaves, wither, and die.

▶ This garbage was left by climbers on Mount Everest. Much of the garbage is plastic, which will never break down but will continue to blow around the mountainside for many years.

EROSION

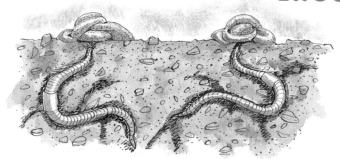

Earthworms help to wear down the mountains. Air and rain travel down the worms' tunnels and break down the rocks below. Fragments of rock come to the surface in the wormcasts and are washed away.

In 1900, forests covered 40 per cent of Ethiopia. Trees were felled, and crops and cattle eroded the bare earth. Today, trees cover only 4 per cent of mountainous Ethiopia, and there are often famines.

SAVING THE MOUNTAINS

In many countries, people have completely changed the nature of their local mountains. In Greece, for example, some forests have been cut down, and sheep and goats have eaten the remaining vegetation. The mountains are reduced to bare rock as the unprotected soil has been completely eroded by wind and rain.

Some countries have created national parks to protect their mountains. Forests are managed so that when one tree is cut down, another is planted. The habitats of wild animals, plants, and birds are protected from damage by people and industry. In this way, mountains can remain areas of great beauty.

All the world's mountains should be protected against long-lasting damage of mining, and logging and the erosion that follows. Mountains play an important role in the earth's weather patterns and support a unique variety of animals and plants.

▲ The yak, or grunting ox, lives on the slopes of the Himalaya in Nepal. These animals have long been used by local people for transport and as a supply of meat and milk. Local people must fight to preserve their traditional ways of life in the mountains.

◄ A volcano rises through the pearly dawn mist in East Java, Indonesia. New volcanoes are formed regularly along fault lines in the earth's crust, while old volcanoes cool and become extinct.

WHAT YOU CAN DO

Support ecology campaigns in these ways:

● There are many groups that campaign to protect mountains and other endangered areas. Find out about their work from magazines and newspapers, on the radio, or on television.

● Tell your friends and relatives about acid rain and mountains in danger.

● Write to your legislators and ask them to fight to protect mountains and help prevent acid rain.

When you go walking or climbing in the mountains, follow these essential rules:

● Use only the marked paths.

● Never pick wild flowers.

● Try not to tread on any plants growing on the mountainside.

HOW COYOTE STOLE FIRE

For thousands of years people have told stories about the world around them. Often these stories try to explain something that people do not understand, like how the world began. This story, told by Native Americans, tries to explain how fire was discovered at the top of a volcanic mountain.

Long ago, when the world was young, Coyote passed by the camp where the People lived. The midday sun was shining on the first snow of winter, and all the People were huddled together in their chilly teepees. It was far too cold to venture out into the world.

"If only we could keep just a little piece of the warm summer sun in our teepees in the winter," said one, wrapping his thick blanket around him more tightly against the draught. He sneezed and looked miserable.

Coyote pitied the People. His own fur grew thick and warm during the winter. Then Coyote had an idea. Perhaps he could help them!

Coyote traveled all the next day to the very top of a nearby mountain. There, in a huddle, sat three fiery creatures, guarding a tiny fire.

As Coyote approached, the three fiery creatures began to sniff the mountain air and look around them suspiciously. They chattered,

"Who's that? Who's trying to steal our fire? Go away!"

When they saw Coyote, the three fiery creatures began to hiss loudly. They stretched out their fiery fingers toward him until he was forced to back off. Then they settled down around the fire again.

But Coyote had not gone very far. He ran off a little way and then crept back and hid behind some bushes to keep watch.

The three fiery creatures spent the whole day guarding the fire but, as night began to fall, two of them disappeared into a nearby cave. A few hours later, the creature left by the fire went to the mouth of the cave and called out to the others.

The second creature soon came out to take his place. Later, the second creature went to the mouth of the cave and called out. This time there was no reply. He called again but still got no answer. Finally, he went right inside the cave, and the fire was left unguarded for a few minutes before the third creature came out.

Coyote watched all this with interest. In fact, he sat watching the fiery creatures for three whole days and nights. Every day, the fire was guarded all the time, except for a few minutes of the night when all three fiery creatures went inside the cave. This was his one chance.

On the fourth night Coyote was ready. When the second fiery creature went into the cave to wake up the third, he ran toward the fire, picked up a flaming branch in his jaws, and dashed off down the steep side of the mountain.

As he ran, he heard the sounds of screaming behind him. The fiery creatures had discovered their loss and were now chasing after him.

Coyote ran and ran, but the fiery creatures were much faster than him. At last one of them came near enough to grab at Coyote's tail. He snatched at it with his fiery hand and scorched the tip of Coyote's tail white. To this day, all coyotes have a white tip to their tails.

When Coyote felt the fiery fingers on his tail, he tossed the flaming branch high into the air. Squirrel leapt down from a tree, grabbed the branch, and ran off down the mountain with it. The fiery creatures followed.

Still they ran too fast. Squirrel felt their burning breath on her back, singeing her fur. To this day, her tail curls up from the scorching heat.

Squirrel threw the branch to Chipmunk, who ran on down the mountain with the fiery creatures close behind.

It took only a few minutes before the fiery creatures began to gain on Chipmunk. He felt the fiery claw of one of them grab at his back, but he wriggled away. And to this day, chipmunks have stripes down their backs from the fiery claw-marks.

Reaching the bottom of the mountain, Chipmunk threw the burning branch to Frog. Poor Frog could not run very fast at all. The fiery beings swept down on him, and one of them grabbed him by the tail. But with one enormous leap, Frog jumped out of the creature's hand, leaving his tail behind. To this day, frogs have no tails.

As soon as he had put some distance between himself and the fiery creatures, Frog threw the flaming branch across to Wood, who swallowed it whole.

The fiery creatures did not know what to do. They were desperate and kicked and scratched and bit at Wood, but he refused to give back their fire. They sat near Wood for four whole days before giving up.

But Coyote knew how to get the fire out of Wood. He taught the People how to twist a stick between their hands with the pointed end rubbing a hole in a piece of wood until a spark appeared. Then the People learned to feed the spark with dry grass until they had a flame. The People could now warm themselves and would never need to be cold again.

TRUE OR FALSE?

Which of these facts are true and which ones are false?
If you have read this book carefully, you will know the answers.

1. The outer layer of the earth is called the mantle.

2. The earth's plates once fitted together like a giant jigsaw puzzle.

3. Mountains cover about half of the earth's surface.

4. Land on a mountainside facing away from the sea often receives very little rain.

5. Alpine flowers are often dull in color to attract local insects.

6. Trees can only survive up to the treeline on the slopes of a mountain.

7. Marmots hibernate all year around and lose most of their body weight.

8. The macaque monkeys of Japan have learned how to cook their food in hot water springs.

9. The Lapps of northern Sweden keep yaks to provide transport, food, and skins.

10. Emeralds are used to make jewelry because of their rich red color.

11. Another name for the grunting ox is the yak.

GLOSSARY

● **Acid rain** is rain polluted by chemicals released from industrial waste, car exhaust, and burning fuel. It can poison trees and plants and erode the face of buildings.

● **Altitude** is the measurement of height above sea level.

● **Avalanche** is caused when heavy snow slips down a mountainside. It can damage property and injure people and animals.

● **Camouflage** hides animals against their surroundings to protect them from predators and can help them capture prey.

● **Coniferous trees** produce cones and are evergreen. They are found mainly in the Northern Hemisphere.

● **Core** is the center of the earth. It is thought to be solid and is likely to be made of iron.

● **Crust** is the name given to the earth's thin surface layer. Mountains are built in the crust.

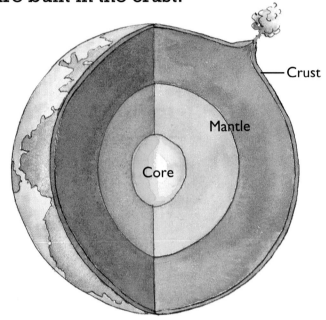

Crust

Mantle

Core

● **Deciduous trees** lose all of their leaves before a cold or dry season. They cannot live in colder climates, as coniferous trees can.

● **Equator** is the imaginary line around the earth, exactly halfway between the North and South poles.

● **Erode** means to wear away. Mountains are eroded by the effects of wind, rain, ice, and snow.

● **Evergreen trees** drop and replace their leaves throughout the year. This means that they always look green. They can grow in colder climates than deciduous trees.

● **Fault-block mountain** is formed when a block of rock is forced up a crack, or fault, in the earth's crust. It often has a flat surface on top, similar to a plain, called a plateau.

● **Fold mountain** is formed when rock is crumpled and forced upward, as the edges of two or more of the earth's plates meet and grind together.

● **Hibernating** is how some animals survive in cold weather. They fatten themselves during the warmer months, then sleep through the long winter.

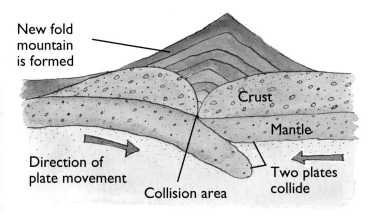

New fold mountain is formed

Crust

Mantle

Direction of plate movement

Collision area

Two plates collide

● **Latitude** is a line drawn from east to west on a map.

● **Mantle** is the layer of rock that surrounds the earth's core and lies beneath the crust.

● **Plate** is one of the huge slabs of rock that make up the earth's crust.

● **Plateau** is the flat area at the top of a block mountain.

● **Predator** is an animal that hunts and kills other animals for food.

● **Rain shadow** is the area on a mountainside facing away from the sea. It receives little rain. Most of the rain falls over the seaward side of the mountain.

● **Snowline** is the level on the side of a mountain above which no plant life can grow. Snow often covers the mountain above this level all year around.

● **Treeline** is the level on a mountainside above which the climate is too cold and windy for trees to grow.

● **Volcano** is an opening in the earth's crust from which very hot, molten rock and gas may leak and cover the surrounding land.

INDEX